HOW BIG IS YOUR WHY?

Author's Guide
to Time Management and
Productivity
to Achieve Transformational Results

I0133577

Marji Hill

Fast Self-Publishing Online, Book 1

First published in 2020 by The Prison Tree Press

    124/1-10 Albert Avenue
    Broadbeach
    Queensland
    Australia 4218

Visit the Marji Hill websites:

    Marjihill.com

    Fastselfpublishing.com

ISBN 13 - 978-0-9924118-2-4

Your Free Bonus

As a small token of thanks for purchasing this book I'd like to offer an exclusive free bonus gift to my readers.

This action packed Free Online Class is called

Discover How To Write A Book Within 30 Days, Publish It On Amazon For Less Than $200, And Get It To Market Within 24 Hours.

It has valuable lessons for those planning to independently publish their book on Amazon.

In this free 45 minutes online class you will learn:

How to create a non-fiction book in 30 days and experience that wonderful sense of achievement

How to self-publish your book a simple, low cost way

How to get your book to market within 24 hours and by applying the fundamentals, start to earn royalties

You can access this free online class HERE

www.fastselfpublishingonline.com

TABLE OF CONTENTS

Chapter 1

Introduction

You want to write a book?

You're ready to write it?

You've gathered together a lot of knowledge, done the research, and you believe you have something to say that will benefit others?

So…

It's time now to put that information out there and be recognised for your expertise.

This publication will seal forever your legacy and will influence the lives of your readers, impact others and maybe even the world.

So why haven't you done it yet?

The truth is, writing a book is scary and there's so much going on in your life.

In your busy life you want to navigate your way to getting your book written and actually completing it.

How Big Is Your Why is designed to help you address your biggest problem…

Time.

Time is your enemy.

In this book I will help you to overcome your challenges with time and you will learn a step-by-step process that will guide you to your destination.

Why am I writing this book?

For many years now I've been interested in how to manage time and, within that 24/7 absolute, how to maximise productivity.

My professional life can be summed up as an entrepreneur who wears three hats –

author,

artist, and

marketer.

As an author I've produced 65 books and still counting.

As an artist I have created a large volume of paintings.

As a marketer I've built a large sales force with a direct selling corporation.

In recent years, I entered the online space and invested heavily in that aspect of my education.

> I learned to build websites and set up multiple social media platforms,
>
> I learned to write blog posts, do affiliate marketing, build email lists, studied automation, and
>
> I learned to make videos and record webinars.

My life has been packed with activity and learning; there's always been so many things I've wanted to do and study, and there was never enough hours in the day to achieve all my passions.

I remember complaining once to my partner saying I wanted to create all these paintings but I just didn't seem to have enough time. His response to me was to learn to manage it.

"If you manage your time well," he said, "you can achieve everything you want in life."

This started my quest into the world of time management and how to maximise my productivity.

Being a highly productive person by nature I have journeyed into learning how to master time. To say that I'm passionate about how to efficiently maximise my output would have to be an understatement.

As we enter 2020, I am sharing with you the insights I have gained about time and how to best manage it in the hope that these insights may help you achieve transformational results.

For you.

The thing about managing your schedule effectively is that you will never be perfect at it. You may do everything you need to do in order to set up your time management system but then it falls apart.

No matter how good at it you become, life has that tendency to always get in the way.

Creativity demands focus, whether it's the book you've always wanted to write, a painting or some other creative pursuit.

It's difficult to give full focus to your creativity when there's a family crisis, lost a loved one, illness, you're recovering from an accident, and the list goes on.

Learn to forgive yourself when trouble or adverse conditions interfere and interrupt your creative pursuits. As the old adage says: "When you fall or fail, get back on the horse".

You will continue to get better at achieving your goals by always striving to improve your mastery over time and learning to maximise your productivity.

Chapter 2

Are you struggling to find time to write?

Most of us are involved in many different projects and find it difficult to allocate a routine time to write.

This is the question that was put to me by one of my students...

> "Does anyone have a system or is it about just being more disciplined?"

Making the most of your time is one of the major challenges facing authors when they are trying to get a book together.

Is time YOUR enemy?

Writers are no different to any other profession or vocation - your day is already filled with other urgencies so how can you find the time to write? A writer's life is busy, busy, busy.

I have a number of friends who are would-be authors and who talk about writing their book.

Most never complete it.

One friend discusses his plans for writing and publishing his short stories every time he visits. This discussion has been going on for a couple of years. I predict that in 10 years' time we will still be having the same discussion.

Another friend has been writing a book. She wrote a few pages and for the past five years she talks about this burgeoning book but she never sits down to write and finish it.

Many people are stranded at the beginning.

They just can't start.

Or they wait for the ideal time.

Or they look for the perfect place to write, their inspiration nook.

Or something else.

Anything, else.

I keep asking the question - why?

The life of a writer, just as it is for other people, is full
of a multitude of priorities:

> working for an income,
>
> raising the kids,
>
> other family commitments,
>
> shopping for the food or that must-have,
>
> education,
>
> recreation,
>
> religious worship,
>
> caring,
>
> housework,
>
> social engagements,
>
> holidays,
>
> watching the cricket,
>
> sport,

exercise…

and the list goes on.

Surprise, surprise… authors too have to constantly juggle their commitments and do battle with unwanted disturbances.

In the middle of all this busyness there are people who desire to write a book. Some have the discipline and they diligently sit down to write while others simply cannot.

When you have so much going on in your life, when your life is so crowded with obligations, how do you schedule in time to write?

A morning person can get up early in the morning and write before the day takes over…

A night person can write at night after everyone else has gone to bed…

…without damaging their health and relationships through lack of sleep.

If finding the time to write is one of your biggest challenges, then you may be surprised to discover that the solution to managing your time lies in your reason for wanting to write.

Chapter 3

How big is your why?

The problem of getting organised and managing your time will resolve when you're clear about your reason to write.

Your motivation.

Some writers, just like artists, say they write when they get the inspiration — so they wait for the muse to magically appear.

As a person, let alone as an artist and a writer, I don't believe in waiting for anything.

My experience is that if you embark on some creative pursuit, inspiration will spring from the sheer act of systematically working on what is in front of you.

The repetitive act of creating a piece of writing or an art work will, in turn, result in inspiration.

For most people, this is counter-intuitive.

But it's axiomatic. The basic premise of your achievement syllogism is you, not something that might happen to or for you.

You can make it happen.

If you develop the habit of writing daily, even for short bursts of time, productivity and creativity will advance.

This in turn creates momentum.

Some say that they can't write at a set time each day.

But who says you can't make an appointment with yourself as you would with a doctor, a lawyer or a candlestick maker?

Mind you, there are others who like the discipline of having a set time to write.

The mere act of writing or painting – being creative – actually doing it and practising it regularly is the source for inspiration.

Inspiration is not some woo-woo mystery…

Inspiration can be generated by practise.

In my experience as an artist, when I'm creating I like to turn out a lot of paintings as quickly as possible.

It's a mistake, I believe, agonising over a single painting and aiming for perfection. It's the frequency of creating that is important.

Some paintings will work well; others not so good.

True inspiration strikes by getting the output happening.

There is a well-known Rugby Union player who is renowned for kicking winning goals. To become that champion he needs strength and accuracy. Anyone watching him would think this success is due to his talent, that it just happens when he is out on the field. He is so good at it.

But no − his inspirational goal kicking comes from years of regimented practise. His mentor advised him that when he is before the roaring crowd, poised and about to kick the goal, that he should clear his mind of anything else and think: "just do it like you do in practise".

This is what astronaut, Neil Armstrong, said when he made his first step onto the moon. When asked what it was like he replied "Just like (it was) in practise".

So practising the craft of writing every day during allocated writing time in turn stimulates and gives impetus to creative thoughts and ideas.

People always find time for the things they want to do.

So if writers are struggling to find the time to write, they need to ask themselves: "why do I want to produce this manuscript?

When the motivation for writing a book is all-powerful, when the reason is something you are really passionate about, the difficulties, the procrastination, the excuses will all disappear.

How big is your why?

Your inner drive will propel your creativity and you will be compelled to move forward.

Nothing will stop you.

Nothing will get in your way.

When you examine the reason for wanting to create a book many of the challenges will resolve if the "why" is big enough. When the "why" is big, you are driven internally and you will pursue your goals relentlessly.

Mastering your time and productivity to get transformational results all starts out with your "why".

What's yours?

Chapter 4

Prioritise

Everyone is busy.

Busy at being busy.

Busy, busy, busy.

People's lives are full of all the things they are obligated to do.

The people who repetitively say they are "gonna write their book" lead active, busy lives. Life gets in the way and they never sit down long enough to focus and produce a manuscript.

They overload their time and do everything else except what they say they want to do, to write.

To start creating a book an author needs to find time in his or her busy life and day to write on a consistent basis.

Step 1 - List your priorities

Once you have clarity on why you are writing a book, the first step to managing your time is to make a list of **all** the activities, responsibilities and commitments in your life.

Do some brainstorming.

Make a mind map.

Toss in everything at random that comes to mind.

Do this with pen and paper, or get some software, an app or some time management tool.

Take a look at this example:

- household chores

- family stuff

- shopping

- exercise

- relaxation time

- ◯ writing

- ◯ sport

- ◯ work for money

- ◯ travel time

- ◯ religious obligation

- ◯ education

Step 2 - Prioritise that list

After the brainstorming, put order into the random jottings.

Prioritise your commitments.

Prioritising the obligations is the major principle behind controlling your time and being more productive.

Identifying the elements that make up the core of your existence and then ranking those commitments helps you to see where you can find time for your creative pursuits.

The task of writing will need to be ranked highly on your list of priorities...

> if your motivation for writing a book is all-powerful,

> when your reason is something you are really passionate about,

> when you are compelled to pursue the writing of your book.

The difficulties, the procrastination, the excuses will all disappear when you ask yourself "how big is your why".

Your book writing goal will become top priority.

Once you know where you categorise your book writing goal, the next step is to prepare a timetable.

Step 3 - Timetable

Generate a 24/7 timetable, get a planner or download an appropriate app.

On the timetable start blocking out units, or chunks of time.

Now name these blocks of time.

Chapter 5

Chunking

How much time do you have?

The maximum available is 7 days a week and 24 hours per day – that is an absolute.

Nothing can change this..

Timetable 24/7

In other words, you don't own any more than 24/7 hours.

Within this absolute, you, as an author, have the opportunity to shine.

When you are totally in control of your 24/7 you can tap into your creative genius and go on to produce your masterpiece.

But the end result, the transformational result you seek, will depend on how good you are at mastering the creative time that is available to you.

Block in your daily and weekly priorities. Block in the time that you relate, sleep, eat, exercise, shop, work, and devote to other commitments.

A key is to name the blocks of time so that it is very clear that you know what you are doing in a particular time slot.

That block of time belongs to that particular task.

In this chunk the aim is to get to a state of heightened and uninterrupted focus so that you can work on either the mundane or creative tasks at hand.

One at a time.

The timetable, or calendar blocking, provides an overview of your week and you'll be able to identify when in that week you can find time to devote to writing.

Can you find 30 minutes, an hour, or two hours of your time that you can dedicate to writing your book?

This time slot could be…

  early in the morning?

  during the day?

  in the evening?

The time you allocate must be your special, sacred and dedicated time.

Daily "to-do" list

Once you have determined what your commitments are for the week and have blocked them into your calendar, you can then create a to-do list for each day.

Plan tomorrow today.

Write down the 6 tasks that have to be completed tomorrow.

Put some order into this list by prioritising them.

You will need to allocate a little bit of your time each day to do this planning so remember to include it on your to-do list.

Beside each task on your list, estimate the time it will take to complete it. This helps to prevent you from getting distracted and doing things that are not relevant to your main purpose.

Timer/alarm

A really useful technique is to put on a timer with an alarm. I frequently use the app on my iPhone.

When I have to complete a task in a given time I set the alarm. This helps to really focus.

Let's say you are working for 60 minutes on what you want to create.

The alarm goes off.

It's time to finish that task and move onto the next one.

This method frees you up mentally so that you are present in the moment. You focus for that particular amount of time on your project.

And only on your project.

It helps to stop the distractions.

Make your next book your top priority

To get the first draft of your manuscript written, I stress that your creative time for writing needs to be top priority.

Whenever I'm writing a book, that's at the top of my daily to-do list. It is the first thing I commit to each day.

I tend to work in two hour blocks of time and do not move on to any other task until I have completed two hours of dedicated writing.

Once your time allocation is completed, you can then move on to the next item on your agenda. Any tasks not completed need to be moved on to the to-do list for the next day.

Otherwise, if they can be overlooked, why were they on your list in the first place?

A priority equals a must-do.

While you are creating the first draft of your book, give it top ranking.

Keep repeating this process daily until you reach your goal and if you do this consistently, you will go nowhere but forward.

Add more power to your productivity by setting yourself a daily word count. If your daily word count goal is 1000 words for 10 days then you will soon complete a 10,000 word draft.

Just remember, as your momentum grows, so does your output and your speed. What started off as a 1000 word goal soon evolves into a minimum word count.

And your enthusiasm fuels your confidence.

Setting dedicated time each day for writing will help you to become laser focussed. In no time you will zoom towards your goal and you will have completed a manuscript.

Chunking tasks

Super-productive people write down their goals for the week.

Prior to each new day they list the six most important tasks to be achieved for tomorrow.

They then identify the most important job that has to be done.

This primary task, sitting at the top priority spot, is best done at the beginning of the day.

Let's say the most important task for the day is to work on the book.

If the book writing is done during the first two hours of the working day, and this practise is done consistently, the manuscript will be completed.

Reaching the goal

Early in my writing career, my partner and I were contracted to produce a critical, annotated bibliography. This project ran for two years.

It was a massive task. We had to review around 1000 books and then write short, critical reviews.

In the first week of the project we had our first set back.

Life got in the way.

I became ill with hepatitis and had it in my system for seven months. But I was determined not to allow this set back interfere with the project.

My approach to getting the work done was this.

Each day I reviewed one book and wrote a short one hundred word review.

I did this consistently.

This daily habit paid off. Little by little we built our bibliography despite my set back. It was like constructing a building brick by brick you might say.

This critical, annotated bibliography went on to become a seminal work in the librarianship niche. It was called *Black Australia: An Annotated Bibliography and Teacher Guide to Resources on Aborigines and Torres Strait Islanders.*

The experience of completing *Black Australia* was my first real lesson in how to maximise productivity despite my initial set back.

Early morning

I start my work day early in the morning. My most productive output happens during those two hours before breakfast.

This is when I write whether it be a book, a blog post, or my social media posting.

It is no secret that many people experience their highest energy and enthusiasm early in the morning. It makes sense, therefore, to allocate the most important and challenging task of the day to be done first thing.

That chunk of time early in the morning is ideal if you are the sort of person who can rise early and get straight into your work.

Chunking for success

Deal with tasks in chunks. Name the task and allocate it to a chunk of time.

For instance, if your goal is to write 1000 words do it within the space of two hours at the start of your working day. Work on that task and strive to reach your word count goal. This is your primary focus.

Avoid doing it only in part and be careful you're not side-tracked by other distractions such as surfing the net or be bombarded by emails and social media.

Mitigate against interruptions or jumping on to another activity by turning off notifications on your devices and making sure your mobile is on silent.

Don't forget to set your timer.

If you divide up your working day up into chunks and then allocate certain tasks to be completed within the allocated periods, you will have more time in your day and you will get more done.

Your working day may be divided into various time slots – 30 minutes, 60 minutes, or 120 minutes – however long you are able to dedicate to your goal. In that time, work only on the chosen task.

Close your door to avoid talking to people. Just focus on the task at hand.

Getting side-tracked and losing focus is easy to do. It's lethal for your concentration if you jump off onto something else.

Skipping from here to there, checking out that link on the internet and then exploring one then another can so easily lead you astray, to losing focus and momentum. Playing solitaire or any other computer game in your dedicated time is simply procrastination.

Suffering overwhelm

Have you ever felt stressed because you seem to have so much to do? You are drowning in what seems an impossible number of enforced priorities, so much so that you suffer overwhelm and begin to feel that you just cannot cope.

I have been there too.

My solution is to begin the chunking process that I have just been talking about.

I brainstorm everything I have to do.

I randomly jot down all the tasks.

I may even mind map them.

Then I put order into this random list.

I start the system of prioritising the list identifying the most important tasks.

I group these into chunks.

Then I estimate how much time each task will take.

As you become practised in time management, you will get better at prioritising the tasks and develop your skills in evaluating the importance of a task.

You will ask if this task is essential to moving forward and reaching your goal. You will assign a heavier weighting to certain tasks and a lesser weighting to something you need to do but which perhaps is not essential at this point in time.

If you practise organising your day based on priorities, your feelings of overwhelm and stress will be alleviated.

The surprising thing is that when you calmly organise your tasks into chunks and then prioritise them, the whole process ceases to become all consuming.

Everything becomes manageable.

You learn to focus on your greater goals rather than being overwhelmed by things of lesser importance and getting lost in the minutiae.

When you reach the end of your working day, review the six tasks you set for the day. Did you achieve all of them?

There is great satisfaction in ticking off the tasks that were successfully achieved. Then if there was anything you didn't achieve, add the task to the next day's list of priorities.

Chapter 6

Best time to write

You may ask "When is the best time of the day to write"? Ultimately, it is you who will decide this.

You will know when you are functioning at your top and when you will feel at your most creative and motivated best.

The tranquillity of early morning may be your preferred time or perhaps late at night may be your peak, creative time when the household has gone to bed and you are still alive and awake.

Choose your optimal time of the day to write and make sure you do it. Do not wait for the ideal time or until conditions are at their best.

Authors who wait for the perfect time never produce anything.

Decide when you will write, block that time into your daily schedule, and just do it.

Seize the day

"Early to bed and early to rise makes a person healthy, wealthy, and wise." These (de-gendered) words of Benjamin Franklin have held true for many distinguished leaders and creators.

Tim Cook, Apple CEO, starts his day at 3.45am. Oprah Winfrey and Michelle Obama are early risers.

Early in the morning there are no major distractions. It's the opportunity to stay ahead of your priorities, and in this quiet, special, and still time you create the space to work on your creativity.

It's the time of day when other people are unlikely to contact you; it's quiet and it's calm; and it's that sacred hour of heightened focus.

Your sacred hour is open to inspiration and creativity. Use those early hours to be on purpose, and to accomplish some amazing things.

Early in the morning, you are less likely to watch television and you probably won't have to turn off your phone — just put it on silent.

During normal working hours

> the phone will ring for sure,

> other people will encroach on your time in some way or other,

> you are easily side-tracked by the demands of social media,

> those emails just keep coming,

and the list goes on.

Without distractions it is easier to focus so you can get your best and most creative work done. But if you have to work in the middle of peak hour interferences and have a problem handling the interruptions, find another environment in which you can write — a library, a park or a coffee shop for example.

The trade off

My world is in motion before sunrise. I wake at 3.30am and I am ready to start work at 4.00am, giving me at least two hours during which I can pursue my goals.

Lots of people are productive in those wee hours around daybreak.

But there is a trade-off.

To do this you need to go to bed earlier.

Everyone needs quality sleep so my rule is to be in bed ready to sleep by 8pm.

If you socialise in the evening or get hooked on television or web surfing and reduce the number of hours that you sleep, then you will find it hard to be at your productive best early in the morning.

How can you expect to function adequately when you feel tired and groggy, even hung over, when you want to perform at peak performance on what is important to you?

At the risk of repeating myself, to have a productive early morning you must ensure that you sleep well.

Or, to put it another way, if you are chronically sleep deprived then the early morning plan is not the best.

Kickstarting the day

When you plan to work early in the morning do something to wake yourself, that is, to energize your body physically. Splash your face with cold water and do some quick physical exercise and/or clap your hands. Get your blood circulating and pump the oxygen to where it's needed most, everywhere.

Getting two or even three hours of productive work done before the day really gets underway always ensures you are moving forward. It kick-starts the day and creates the momentum you need.

Even if things outside your control crop up during the day, and they do, you can be comforted in the knowledge that at least you have accomplished some writing no matter what.

When your work environment is busier and your attention is challenged with competing interruptions, it becomes harder and harder to have the will power to block out the distractions.

During those early hours, work on what is most important to you, like your writing, getting that 1000 words written or a chapter completed or edited.

Work on what you are most passionate about so that when the rest of the household is sleeping you are at full focus and concentration.

My message to you is to identify the time of the day when you function at your best and dedicate this time to your most important task, writing your manuscript.

And in this special time, block out the diversions like Facebook, your email, or anything else that is going to challenge your ability to focus.

Chapter 7

Classic drains on your time

I love this quote from Warren Buffett: "The difference between successful people and very successful people is that very successful people say 'no' to almost everything".

If you are developing a mastery with managing your time, identify the classic drains on your success.

What steals your time?

Here are some of the main time-wasters:

Emails

I always hear people complain about how they get too many emails and that reading and responding to them is time consuming. Dealing with emails is one of those daily activities that can drain your day and play havoc with your productivity.

Maybe you are one of those who dreads logging into their email because the chore is overwhelming. Emails can and will flood your inbox.

If you don't manage your emails, this task can easily become one of your greatest time wasters. Emails do have to be checked, that's for sure, but you have to guard against become a slave to them.

Avoid having your email program open all the time. Instead have a set time each day to check your emails and try to deal with them quickly.

You don't want to read and respond to every email. It eats too much into your time.

Learn to control your emails rather than having them control you. Make quick decisions. Which are the important ones?

Quickly sort and file them into appropriate categories and delete those that are unimportant.

Meetings

Meetings are notorious for draining time. I've always hated meetings and for most of my working life I've done my very best to avoid them except when they are absolutely essential.

Always consider whether or not a meeting is important. Perhaps an email or a phone call is a good alternative. Remember that face-to-face can also be achieved with tele-conferencing and there are numerous free programs that can assist you.

Perfectionism

I've come across a number of authors who want to produce a book but they let their need for perfectionism get in the way of their productivity. By trying to be perfect they set very high standards which they can never attain.

Authors should get their rough draft done as quickly as possible. You should be prepared to accept the fact that your first attempt will be imperfect. Later you can come back to rework the manuscript and refine your draft.

It usually takes several revisions before your masterpiece is ready for public consumption, no matter how "perfect" the first draft.

Facebook

Facebook would have to hold the current time-honoured position for being the most effective distraction to steal your time.

Being the notorious time waster it is, having your Facebook tab open while you are writing is simply asking for trouble. Facebook is compulsive and you can become obsessed with checking Facebook almost every minute of the day.

Getting distracted by Facebook or other social media is dead easy. I've done it myself many a time and fallen into its trap.

Others making demands on your time

Other people demand attention and can encroach upon your time.

> The visitors who decide to drop in and absorb your time.

> The household members, your family, who claim your attention.

The possibilities can be endless unless you do something about it.

It doesn't stop there

In addition there arc many other time wasters:

> organising files on your computer,

> television,

> watching movies,

> YouTube,

> televised sporting events...

Sound familiar? What's your favourite procrastination aid?

You have to set the boundaries for when and how you will allow the distractions to impinge on the one precious commodity you can never replace, your time.

Now for a time audit

To create awareness of where your day disappears, you need to track what you actually do throughout the day, an audit.

You already have your 24 hour chart (if not, please revise Chapter 3) but an audit is something different. An audit ensures you are not fooling yourself into believing that seductive dream world where you think you are doing your best is actually real.

From time to time, create another 24 hour chart and break this down into 30 minute time slots. A time management app may help.

Now fill it in with everything you do making sure you leave nothing out.

Be brutal.

How long were your meals?

How long was it between sitting at your desk and beginning your work?

How many coffee breaks?

How many toileting breaks?

Did you time your phone calls or just make an estimate?

Track EVERYTHING you do over a 24 hour period.

Do this for a week.

Boring?

Yes.

Essential?

Yes. Yes. Yes.

People say to me that they are so busy - busy, busy, busy - and that they work very hard. But there can be a very big discrepancy between what they think they do and what they actually do.

It is essential to identify the things in your daily life that are eroding your time.

What's draining *your* time?

Who or what's stealing your time?

> Is it your family pouring through the open door to your work space?
>
> How many calamities did you have to deal with?
>
> Were you distracted by a news event on television?
>
> Or a sporting event?
>
> Do visitors drop in unannounced?
>
> Are you always surfing the net or getting distracted by social media?

Learn to say "No".

If social commitments become a pressure and shrink your time, learn to say something like "Let me take a look at my diary and I'll get back to you".

Like it or not, you need to evaluate invitations and social commitments. If you disagree, maybe it's time to revise Chapter 3 (How big is your why?).

Make some decisions and prioritise the important ones.

Conclusion

I trust you've got a number of tips about time management.

So to achieve transformational results, focus on how you are spending the time you have available. If you master your time well, you will be able to create a life balance.

It won't be always about sacrificing the activities you like to do. Your book will get written when you achieve time mastery.

When you manage your time successfully, and practise it, you will make time to pursue your creativity. You will become more productive and you will still include your life's obligations and have time for some rest and recreation.

The top secret of time management rests in:

> understanding why you are pursuing a creative goal, such as finishing your manuscript, and
>
> learning to prioritise tasks. What will drive you forward to your ultimate goal is this ability to know what is important to you, selecting the key one and doing it.

This is the transformational outcome you can achieve.

You will learn to eliminate what is irrelevant and you will have the mental space to move forward in your quest for productivity.

In managing my own time I keep asking myself this question: "what tasks do I need to do tomorrow that will propel me towards my goal?"

If you fail to do this you will likely feel "busy" all the time. Many activities may not align with your ambitions so it's possible to waste much of your valuable time on petty matters that do not move you forward on the path you want to travel.

Your life-goals are important to you.

Don't let anyone or anything steal them.

Sources

Glei, Jocelyn K *Manage Your Day-to-Day: Build Your Routine, Find Your Focus, and Sharpen Your Creative Mind.* Amazon Publishing. Kindle Edition, 2013.

Penn, Joanna *Productivity for Authors.* Curl Up Press, 2019

Rampton, John   8 Biggest Time Wasters That Kill Your Productivity *https://www.inc.com/john-rampton/8-time-wasters-that-kill-your-productivity.html*

Reh, F. John   Why Chunking Is Better Than Multitasking for Improving Work Efficiency *https://www.thebalancecareers.com/dont-multi-task-when-you-can-use-chunking-2276184*

About Marji Hill

MARJI HILL is an Australian author.

Marji was born in Surfers Paradise on Queensland's Gold Coast. In her writing career she has published more than 65 titles on all aspects of Indigenous Australia, other Australian ethnicities, and self-improvement.

Many of her books have been for children and young adults.

In 2014 Marji branched out into the self-improvement niche with Staying Young Growing Old.

Apart from being a writer Marji is also an artist.

Reconciliation

In all of her professional life, Marji has been writing books to promote understanding between Indigenous and Non-Indigenous Australians. She has fostered the spirit of Reconciliation in all her work since she was Research Fellow in Education at the Australian Institute

of Aboriginal and Torres Strait Islander Studies
(AIATSIS) in Canberra.

In 1989 Marji was the Project Co-ordinator and one of
the researchers and writers of *Australian Aboriginal
Culture* the official Australian Government publication
on Aboriginal Australians and Torres Strait Islanders.

Six Australian Battlefields

In 1988 her work of non-fiction *Six Australian
Battlefields*, which she co-authored with Al Grassby,
was published by Angus and Robertson. A decade later
it was republished by Allen & Unwin as a paperback.

The 9 volume encyclopaedia, *Macmillan Encyclopaedia
of Australia's Aboriginal Peoples* was published in 2000
and in 2009 Marji published *The Apology: Saying Sorry
to the Stolen Generations*.

Marji has a Master of Arts specialising in Anthropology
from the Australian National University.

Professional artist

Marji is also a professional artist. One of her large oil paintings was included in the 2004-2005 Ballarat Fine Art Gallery Travelling Exhibition *Eureka Revisited: the Contest of Memories*. This exhibition travelled to Melbourne, Canberra and Ballarat – part of the 150 years celebration of the Eureka Stockade.

Another of her paintings was in the foyer of Jupiter's Casino in Townsville while her portrait of Jupiter Mosman hangs in the World Centre at Charters Towers in North Queensland. These two paintings celebrate the story of Indigenous boy, Jupiter Mosman, who discovered gold at Charters Towers in 1871.

Marji's paintings arc held in many private collections in Australia and overseas. She is represented in collections at Ballarat Fine Art Gallery and the Australian Catholic University.

As part of her professional work, Marji has travelled throughout Aboriginal Australia and the Torres Strait.

Fast Self-Publishing Online

Given Marji's long and extensive experience in the book industry, she is now sharing her knowledge and expertise with people who want to write and self-publish. She is the founder of Fast Self-Publishing Online the platform she uses to coach and help authors.

More Books from Marji Hill

Self-improvement:

Hill, Marji (2014) Staying Young Growing Old. Broadbeach, Qld, The Prison Tree Press.

Aboriginal Australia:

Hill, Marji (2017) First People Then and Now: Introducing Indigenous Australians. Broadbeach, Qld, The Prison Tree Press.

Marji Hill (2018) First People Then and Now: Australian Aboriginal Heroes of the Resistance Broadbeach, Qld, The Prison Tree Press.

What do you think?

What do you think of *How Big Is Your Why: An Author's Guide to Time Management and Productivity to Achieve Transformational Results?*

First of all, I really appreciate the fact that you purchased my book.

Thank you. I am extremely grateful.

I hope that *How Big Is Your Why* has added value and provided you with quality information about managing your time and being more productive as an author.

It would be really nice if you could share your enthusiasm for this book with your friends and family by posting on Facebook or other social media.

If you enjoyed this book and found some benefit in reading it, I'd really appreciate it if you could take a little bit of your time to post a review on Amazon.

I want you, the reader, to know that your review is very important and so, if you'd like to leave a review, all you have to do is...

> **Open Amazon and go to *HOW BIG IS YOUR WHY? An Author's Guide to Time Management and Productivity to Achieve Transformational Results***
>
> **Click *Ratings***
>
> **Click *Review this product***

I wish you all the best in your future success!

Thank you

www.ingramcontent.com/pod-product-compliance
Lightning Source LLC
Chambersburg PA
CBHW071024040426

42443CB00007B/921